how to make
working from home
work for
you

Everything you need to know about
working from home effectively

Rachael Ross
Foreword by Philip Smith, Home Business Network

Published by Filament Publishing Ltd
14, Croydon Road, Waddon,
Croydon, Surrey CR0 4PA
Telephone 020 8688 2598
www.filamentpublishing.com

"How to make working from home work for you"
by Rachael Ross

ISBN 978-1-905493-28-9

Printed by Antony Rowe, Eastbourne
Distributed by Gardners Books

Cover design & illustrations Natalie Piper
Photography Charlotte Emery
Copywriter Jackie Barrie

Reviews

'I am a advocate of having an home based office and 'How to make working from home work for you' is an essential guide. Teaching you what you need to know and what it is really like to work from home.

Sahar Hashemi
Entrepreneur, co-founded Coffee Republic
Turned best-selling author.
www.anyonecandoit.co.uk

As someone based at home and who coaches others around home based businesses I will definitely be recommending 'How To Make Working From Home Work For You" to my clients! The practical exercise of noting changes to implement, ensures the reader takes responsibility for their actions.

I have started to implement one suggestion already. Since I work from a limited area, it is vital that I only have what is essential in arms reach. So all the extra files and folders are now in my document storage cupboard; easy to get to but no longer taking up important space or causing a distraction... amazing how these simple little things can make a difference to productivity!

Yvonne Bignall,
Director
EHO Coaching Limited
www.ehocoachingltd.com

Canadian organisation and efficiency guru, Rachael Ross, has just had her first book published in the UK, 'How To Make Working From Home Work For You'. The book is a step-by-step, desk-top learning guide with key chapters laid out with check-lists to help focus the mind and encourage the reader to actually think about how to accomplish things.

Not only does the book look at the home working environment, but also that most important element of all - yourself. Several chapters look at honing that personal performance, which makes this guide for us, significantly more beneficial than many other titles in the sector.

The emphasis is bang on, in our view; without the right frame of mind you can't even 'bring it all together', as Rachael says.

Rachael also looks carefully at the balance between a professional performance and the lifestyle benefits of working from home. Getting it just right can be very difficult and this book tackles the issues which need to be addressed and how.

All written in a friendly, open and clutter-free style, this book is an arms-length must-have for your home office and we will certainly be recommending it to our members.

Len Tondel
Director
Home Business Alliance
www.homebusiness.org.uk

Home-working adviser Rachael Ross has encapsulated her advice for struggling home-based workers in a commonsense guide. Ross' book is aimed at those new to the game, and those who are finding it less than easy going. The book is set out in easily digested chunks, with commonsense solutions to many of the perceived disadvantages of home-working.

Ross' real strength is her structured approach to personal discipline, so there are sensible suggestions for creating a physical environment conducive to work, achieving the right frame of mind and scheduling your work programme

Lisa Thompson
Editor
www.liveworkhomes.co.uk

As Rachael says. If it suits you, working from home can "boost productivity and improve work/life balance, benefiting you, your employer, your business and your lifestyle. To make this happen she advises on how to make it clear to family and friends that your workspace and work time must be respected. And to draw a line between home and work life so that you are not always caught between the two.

Julie McCarthy
Publisher
www.familyinterest.co.uk

This book is dedicated to
Daniel Walberg Fuglesang, who always
challenged and encouraged me.
You are loved and always will be missed.

Foreword

We are all well aware that thousands of small and medium-sized firms form the backbone of the UK economy out there. And we know that more people work for such organisations than the high profile corporate.

But few of us are aware of just how many of those businesses are based at home, and how great a role that sector will play in the economic revival. It's quite amazing really, just how many long running and successful businesses are based at the owner's home, ranging from one-man trades to companies employing tens of staff.

Yet it's a sector that has been largely ignored... until now. *How to make working from home work for you* will show would-be and established home workers how to make the most of the huge benefits of working from home – whether it's the spare room or garden shed.

This book is also a great help for those looking to avoid the pit-falls and has a wealth of advice on such critical issues as keeping the neighbours on side, selecting the correct IT equipment and maintaining a structured and clutter-free, and hence productive, environment.

It's tough working from home. You need discipline, dedication and drive. It's not for everyone, but if it is for you, then the following pages will be invaluable.

Philip Smith
Editor
Home Business Network
www.homebusinessnetwork.co.uk

Acknowledgement

There are several people I would like to acknowledge and say a big thanks to for all their help and support throughout the development of this book.

Copywriter
Jackie Barrie
Comms Plus
www.comms-plus.co.uk

Cover design
Natalie Piper
natpiper@live.co.uk

Kelly Ross, my brother and a talented amateur.

Illustrations
Natalie Piper
natpiper@live.co.uk

Photo (back cover)
Charlotte Emery
SEA Photography
ww.seaphotography.com

Proof reading
Tanya Clarke
Aspects Virtual Solutions
www.aspectsvirtualsolutions.co.uk

*Names of clients have been changed to protect their anonymity.

Contents

Contents

Introduction…
How to make working from home work for you

I'm looking at a cartoon of a girl sitting in a bubble-bath with her mobile phone to her ear. It's headed, 'Working from home helped her focus on the really important projects' and she's saying, 'Blah blah shoes blah blah di blah, let's do lunch darling, I need a new outfit, blah blah di blah blah'.

Meanwhile, somewhere in the world, at least one office manager is wondering whether his staff are currently slaving away in their home offices or skiving off with magazines, daytime TV, computer games or social networking websites.

That's the stereotypical image of home-working.
But it doesn't have to be that way.

Being based at home allows you to establish a working environment that best suits your working style, and by making quick adjustments you can increase your effectiveness. It can also boost productivity and improve work/life balance, benefiting you, your employer, your business and your lifestyle.

As an expert in effective home-working, I've helped hundreds of people turn their badly behaved home offices into organised and efficient work spaces with productive workflow processes. In this book, I address the benefits and the difficulties of working from home and share my tried-and-tested tips and success secrets.

My previous career was in design and tailoring, so I know how you have to cut your cloth according to your needs. Similarly, no one solution fits all home-workers. In this book I pose many questions and provide many answers. Work through the book to find out what suits you best, so that:

- Family members will respect your work space
- Friends will know not to interrupt you when you're working
- You set up your office space in the best way for you
- You create a successful *frame of mind*
- You develop working habits that enable you to accomplish more
- You master time-management
- You won't be checking your e-mails at midnight
- You draw a line between work and home life
- Your clients will perceive you as professional
- You won't be tempted to stop work and put the washing in or watch the footie
- Your boss will respect the work you deliver
- You find out whether you're a 'filer' or a 'piler' and arrange your paperwork accordingly

Whether you already work from home or you're just thinking about it, whether you run your own business or work for an employer, whether you work full-time or part-time, there's plenty of useful advice in this book for you.

P.S. Working from home is an increasingly popular option for employers, employees and self-employed workers for various reasons. I'm writing this book at a time when the economy is wobbly and everyone is more financially aware. So I've included a bonus chapter with money-saving tips you just can't afford to ignore.

Rachael Ross

purely
peppermint
The Home and Office Organising Expert

Chapter 1
Working from home...does it work?

The idea of working from home sounds like a wonderful dream to many people. It could be the ideal working environment you have been longing for, but does it sound like a dream you could turn into a reality?

What would it be like if your commute was only one minute and you never had to struggle through the hoards of commuters on public transport, or sit in a traffic jam? What would it be like if you were able to work the hours that suit you best and not the hours set by head office? What would it be like to be your own boss? If this sounds like the ideal way to work, you now need to ask these questions :

Would I like to work from home?
and
Could I do it successfully?

An example of how it can successfully work is sisters Emily and Sophie. They are a dynamic web design team who with my help have made their dream of working from home become a reality. Initially the idea was something they had thought would suit them well, but just didn't know how to pull it all together. Now they are enjoying:

> A more relaxed start to their day, made possible by no longer having to commute

➤ Flexibility in their schedule which allows them to fulfil family responsibilities as their mother now needs extra care, sometimes involving regular hospital visits. With Emily and Sophie being in control of their schedule, one or both can be available when their mother needs their help

➤ A more conducive working environment. Emily was easily distracted by colleagues and found it difficult to complete projects when working in a buzzing and noisy office. This resulted in her feeling under pressure and stressed. Now Emily and Sophie have established ground rules that during certain important tasks Emily is left to work free from interruptions. This has resulted in lower stress levels and higher productivity for Emily

Yes, a home office can be the perfect place to allow the flexibility needed when creating your most harmonious and productive working environment. With that in mind, here is another question that needs to be asked:

Can working from home realistically work for everybody?

Are you self-motivated with enough dedication to carry on working even when there isn't someone looking over your shoulder?

Will the extra time you gain by no longer needing to commute be put to good use and not just squandered away?

Can you realistically say that you will be more productive and successful working from home?

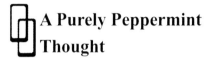 **A Purely Peppermint Thought**

Since so many tasks are computer based these days the question posed is:

Can these tasks be achieved as successfully from a home office as they can be from the traditional office building?

The answer is YES

As you continue to read the rest of this book you will discover dozens of tips and techniques that will ensure that you make working from home a success.

Now we need to look at whether working from home can work for you.

I have many clients who prove that working from home can suit a wide range of people. First you must have a willingness to implement any changes necessary and eliminate work practices which are currently letting you down. You also need to understand your strengths and weaknesses, when it comes to being based at home. And, importantly remember to incorporate your family and their needs into how you structure your day. More on all of that later.

Benefits and drawbacks

With any decision there are benefits and drawbacks and work-ing from home is no different. Throughout this chapter we will consider the benefits and drawbacks of *working from home,* but rest assured in the knowledge that for any drawback there is a solution.

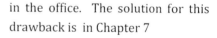 If the benefit you are looking forward to is to be your own boss, the drawback may be that you are now responsible for looking after everything, even the areas in which you are not an expert. The result could be that you are now spending too much time doing tasks you don't enjoy and not the job that brings in the money. You will find solutions for this drawback in Chapter 6

 Another benefit you may be excited to experience is having more time with the family but that may result in even more interruptions at home than when you were in the office. The solution for this drawback is in Chapter 7

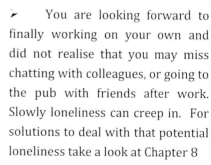 You are looking forward to finally working on your own and did not realise that you may miss chatting with colleagues, or going to the pub with friends after work. Slowly loneliness can creep in. For solutions to deal with that potential loneliness take a look at Chapter 8

Further benefits you could enjoy:

- Flexibility to schedule your day according to your needs
- Improved quality of life
- Improved productivity
- Saving on the start up costs
- Reduced stress
- A healthier lifestyle

Not only are there benefits to entrepreneurs or employees based at home, there are also benefits for organisations that encourage home working amongst their employees.

An organisation could benefit by:

- Having higher staff retention
- Reduced overheads
- Increased pool of potential recruitment applicants
- Less absenteeism
- Increased profits

If you feel you could work effectively from home and want your employer to consider the possibility, start by compiling information to pull together a proposal. There are a couple of areas it should include. First, show that you can work successfully and effectively from home (including how you will ensure your focus is on work and not distracted by family). And second, show how the organisation will benefit by allowing you to change your office to a new home location (it could something like saving the company money, or an increase in your focus).

Why do you want to Work from Home?

The decision regarding whether or not you are going to work from home is not a quick rash idea, but rather a purposeful choice. This is a choice made through careful consideration, research and investigation. I have just explored some of the benefits and potential drawbacks you may experience when working from home. The next step is to consider the reasons behind why you want to be based at home in the first place.

> Is it because there is a career or business opportunity of which you want to take advantage?

> Is it because you want to reduce stress and bring a little balance into your life?

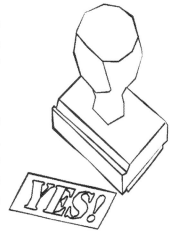

> Is it because you are starting a company and working from home is the most cost effective way to get your business off the ground?

> Is it because you want to enjoy having control over your work schedule and be more available for the family?

> Is it because you want establish a work environment more suitable to your needs?

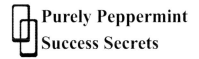

Purely Peppermint Success Secrets

Since you are making a purposeful choice,
don't assume that you can work in a random manner
without establishing
a proper structure and effective systems.

Such a style of working will lead to chaos, frustration and far
too much stress.

To help with your purposeful choice, you need to see whether working from home is even possible.

Think about:

- How will it affect the rest of the family?
- Is your job conducive to it?
- Do you have the space in your home?
- Can you keep work and home life separate?

When Hannah was looking at getting back into teaching, she gave me a call. Originally the possibility of working from home was never considered until an online teaching position became available. We were working though the process of making a *purposeful choice* when it became clear to Hannah that this was her ideal scenario. Not only would she be working in an area she loved, but the flexibility in the schedule meant she could be there for her children before and after school.

Personality traits

Earlier I referred to the happy realisation that working from home can suit most people but only **you** will know if it will suit you. There are a variety of personality traits and skills that are beneficial when working from home.

A few of the skills or personality traits you need:

- To be able to work well as an individual
- To be self motivated
- To be able to manage your time
- To be hard working and focused
- To be confident in your abilities
- To be able to set goals
- To be able to self-discipline
- To be able to create a schedule and follow it
- To be able to evaluate situations and make quick decisions
- To be able to communicate well

Of course, you may not have every single attribute and skill, but by using the traits you have and being willing to ask for help in the areas that are not your strength or expertise, you will have success.

> **Throughout this book I will be covering tips, advice and tried and tested solutions, for every home working situation.**
>
> **So read on…..**

The different home working sectors

The working from home sector can be separated into different categories, these can include small business owners and full time employees. But also individuals who work from home a few days of the week, while the rest of the time they are either at head office or on the road.

Entrepreneur/Self Employed

Such people usually have the most flexibility in their working day; however they also need to possess a highly developed self motivation muscle. Being your own boss can have a down side as everything hangs on your shoulders. It is unlikely that there is a back up team, so it will be necessary for you to create your own support system with other business owners and experts.

Employee

An employee works for an organisation and usually has someone back at the main office to whom they need to report. There are many similarities with an entrepreneur in how best to work from home but also subtle differences in the structure of your day, what tasks you need to work on, and other specific requirements that are going to be set by your employer.

Part time

No matter how many days you are based at home, there is still so much to learn from this book about working successfully. Part time individuals need to have an organised and structured set up to their day and working space, especially since you need to shift from 'home mode' to 'work mode' quickly and easily. There will be more about the shift between 'home and work mode' in Chapter 4.

More points to consider

The neighbours

You must never overlook how important it is to make sure you keep everything OK with the neighbours.

Be mindful of:

- ➤ If you are going to receive clients at your home, is there ample parking for residents and visitors?

- ➤ Are you going to be making more noise than usual which might annoy any of the neighbours who are home during the day?

- ➤ Are you making any renovations to your property or an outbuilding that may affect a neighbour?

If a neighbour complains about the fact that you are using your residence as a base for work, it could be the end of working from home. So be considerate and respect their feelings and needs.

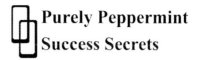

Purely Peppermint Success Secrets

There is no 'one' perfect way to work from home. It can all depend on the job you do, the space you have, your

Insurance and mortgage

Make sure to inform both the insurance company and mortgage provider that you are working from home. They will ask you questions specific to the policy you currently have, so be sure that your answers are completely honest to avoid any issues later on.

If you receive clients or customers, it is recommended that you also take out public liability insurance to protect yourself in case anyone suffers an injury while at your home office.

The lessons you have learned.

What are the first three action steps you will take to help with your purposeful choice?

1._____

_____

_____

_____

2._____

_____

_____

_____

3._____

_____

_____

_____

Chapter 2
The Home Office

Imagine that after a successful negotiation with your boss there is an opportunity to work at home. The spare room will become your office, the family are on board with you now being based at home and you are looking forward to the change and improving your working environment.

But now what?

Or.....

You have a brilliant business idea and plan to venture out to start your very own home based company. With the excitement building, you have written a business plan, hired a website designer and ordered the business cards.

But what should you do next?

To start turning the dream into a reality and pull it all together, you need to set up and organise your work space including an efficient office.

> **You are not going to establish that efficient,**
> **office or working area**
> **without**
> **first considering what your needs will be.**

Planning

When I originally spoke to Noah, he was showing signs of being stressed because his partner, Jessica, recently started working from home. She had 'set up camp' (as he called it) on the kitchen table and was leaving her papers and mess all over the room. For Noah, the arrangement **was not working.** This came as no surprise to me because the issue of how an office location and the affect it will have on the family is one I deal with frequently. And for Noah and Jessica it also affected their relationship and brought unwanted stress into their lives.

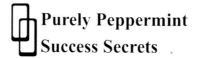 **Purely Peppermint Success Secrets**

Prior Planning and Perfect Preparation Prevents Poor Performance.

This situation was straight forward to sort out as they were in the fortunate situation of having a spare room. Up to this point the room was full of clutter, boxes and an unused broken futon.

First off we set about our ***planning*** by looking at what Jessica's job entails, the equipment she needed, and how she was going to structure her working day. With all the information that was gathered we were able to put together a great little office. Now Jessica has an effective office and Noah's stress has vanished.

This is when you start planning your own office requirements. Where would the best location be? If it is going to be part of a room which has another function already, you could look into alternative office structures such as a hideaway office computer cabinet. These can be easily closed away at the end of the day.

You also need to consider:

♦ How much space is needed?
♦ Is there enough storage?
♦ Will the room maintain a comfortable temperature?
♦ Do you need a space separate from the family?
♦ What type of office will allow you to work at your best?
♦ Does it have internet access?
♦ Is there enough light?
♦ Can you comfortably meet clients in this space?
♦ Do you need desk space for an employee?
♦ Will the room have more than one use?
♦ Do you have enough electrical outlets?
♦ Will you have enough privacy?

Remember there is **no 'one' perfect way to work from home.**

The key is to set up an office to suit your own individual needs and working style.

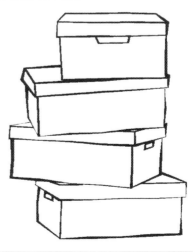

Creating your own perfect office space will depend on **the type of home you live in.**

- ◆ Are you able to designate a room as your office?
- ◆ Is there space for a new shed/office in your garden?
- ◆ Are you able to convert the loft?
- ◆ Will your office be part of a multi functioning room?

If your office is going to be part of another room, how will you keep the two uses separate? And on the topic of keeping spaces separate, one point to remember is that no matter where you set up your office you need to make sure it remains contained in the office area and doesn't spread into other parts of the house. One of the key features of working successfully from home is in keeping the two functions of your home separate.

When space is tight, consider other possibilities. Are you able to convert the loft to give you an extra room? Is there an empty outbuilding on your property that can be upgraded into a nice spacious private office? Do you have room in your garden for a purposely designed *home office/shed*? I have worked with a client whose garden office is the envy of all home workers. And now there is a brand new garden office possibility on the market known as the OfficePOD®. It is a self contained, stylish, eco friendly, secure POD that gives you the space needed to work productively.

Don't get caught up in the traditional thought pattern of what an office should be like. Look into all the possibilities available and choose the one that will suit you best.

Your perfect way of working from home can also **depend on the type of job you do.**

- ♦ Will you be working from a desk using a computer?
- ♦ Will you be receiving clients?
- ♦ Do you need space to store product samples?
- ♦ Will you need the use of a separate treatment room?
- ♦ Do you need space for a drawing table ?
- ♦ What are the health and safety requirements?

Consider your answers to the previous questions. They will influence your storage needs and how best to set up the space. There are also various office supplies to consider (more info in the next chapter). But for now.

Office supplies

An average office may need some or all of the following:

- ♦ Desk, chair
- ♦ Computer work station
- ♦ Computer, printer, fax
- ♦ Scanner, photocopier
- ♦ Calendar, clock
- ♦ Stationery supplies
- ♦ Shredder
- ♦ Sufficient lighting
- ♦ Filing cabinet and shelves, storage area
- ♦ Anything specific to your individual needs

Before you buy any products or supplies, Remember:

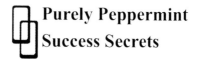

Purely Peppermint Success Secrets

Going out and buying every organising piece of equipment and storage container will not make you organised and wastes money.

You need to decide what your filing, storage and office requirements are, so that you can buy wisely.

Remember that once the office is set up and systems are in place you need to file, organise and de-clutter on a regular basis to maintain an organised, effective office.

Health and Safety

It is important to remember that your home office is also subject to Health and Safety regulations.

- ◆ Is the equipment correct for the job that is being done?
- ◆ Is your chair comfortable, adjustable and with adequate back support?
- ◆ Is the keyboard placed at the correct height?
- ◆ Is the screen positioned free from any potential glare?

Take a look at the health and safety guideline booklet, available from the Health & Safety Executive. Their contact details are in the *useful contacts* section at the end of the book.

Technology

It continually surprises me how often a client will say, 'I bought the latest Blackberry or the latest online program or a filing cabinet, but I just can't seem to get organised', and then look at me in despair. They do not yet fully understand my previous success secret about the fact that things do not make you organised but taking action will.

One of my favourite clients Jamie had several boxes full of every organising gadget, device and contraption known to man. There were some I didn't even know existed. She never took the time to learn how to use a single gadget as most of the instruction booklets and power supplies were lost. The result was a disorganised Jamie who had wasted time and money.

The first step towards Jamie achieving any productivity was for her to promise that she would never again be tempted by an organising gadget. Jamie realises how impractical all the purchases had been and since taking action she is now enjoying a clutter free, organised office.

Technology has changed and improved so much that a whole new world of possibilities has opened up. Especially for anyone who previously thought working from home was only a pipe-dream.

What equipment or communication tools are going to help you work effectively and stay in touch with colleagues, customers or clients? Using technology can help with combating your potential feelings of isolation and at the same time open your business up to worldwide marketing possibilities.

Technology available:

- A mobile phone with e-mail and web access
- Answering machine/service
- Call forwarding
- Webcam
- Video conferencing
- Skype
- WiFi
- Remote access to your company's digital information
- Digital camera
- Almost daily new and exciting developments

In the past couple of years the digital camera has increased my business and brought me clients from all over the country and world. The process starts when they send me photos of their badly behaved offices. After studying such photos we have a telephone consultation to find specific and clear-cut solutions for any of the *working from home* issues they find challenging.

Look into the technology available and see what you can find that will help in a way you never thought possible.

The lessons you have learned.

What are the first three action steps you will take that will help you plan and set up your home office?

1._____

_____

_____

_____

2._____

_____

_____

_____

3._____

_____

_____

_____

Chapter 3
Effective Storage

There is nothing quite like a well maintained organised filing and storage area to help you work effectively from home.

No matter the size of your home office, I cannot emphasise enough the value of establishing a systematic, organised filing and storage strategy. It is always satisfying to help clients with this area, because having your filing, storage and paperwork in order is one of the most powerful ways to initiate change and improve a chaotic office and working situation.

In this chapter I will be looking at the different types of filing equipment and storage options available. Later on in the book there is advice looking at the administration side of running an organised office and all the fun involved in dealing with the *nitty gritty* aspect of filing and paperwork.

In the previous chapter it was discovered that unfortunately all the storage containers and organising equipment in the world will not guarantee instant organisation. You need to establish a storage/paperwork system and maintain it regularly; more on that next.

What do you need to store?

- Mainly paperwork
- Instruction manuals
- Bulky products
- Computer equipment or business machinery
- Training handbooks
- Product samples
- Reference material
- Even more paperwork

De-clutter

I could not cover the topic of storage without examining the all important step of de-cluttering; sorting and clearing any items that are having a detrimental effect on your environment. De-cluttering the office will allow you to realise what your storage requirements are. This process saves money because now you will only purchase the storage products you need.

It is amazing how your motivation and energy levels increase when you are working in an office that has been de-cluttered and only contains the items you require to work at your best.

One piece of advice I have for you is this; when you start a large de-cluttering and organising session, **the space will look worse before it gets better,** just as when you redecorate a room. Don't be discouraged because this situation is only a temporary stop on the road to a brighter, organised future.

Tips for dealing with paperwork:

> Set aside plenty of time

> Have a positive mood. You should never de-clutter when you are angry, sad or frustrated, just as you should never go grocery shopping when you are hungry

> Sort paperwork into two piles, *Current* and *Archive*

> Streamline the archive pile. Now you will know how much storage is needed for the remaining archived paperwork

> Streamline the current pile. What needs to be kept? Is there anything that can be stored electronically? What types of containers and how many do you need?

The best way to finish off a paperwork session is to shred everything that holds any personal information.

I will be going into more detail regarding **productive home working habits** and dealing with day to day paperwork and office systems in Chapter 5.

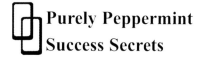

**Purely Peppermint
Success Secrets**

**To establish a well organised storage and filing
system, you need to choose the
best, biggest and most effective
*Storage cabinets,
Boxes,
Shelves,
Drawers,
Filing system,*
available for the space you have and the
amount of items that are to be stored.**

Paperwork storage

Your paperwork storage does not always have to end up with opting for the traditional filing cabinet, if that doesn't work best with your office space or your organising style. There is a wide variety of products available for you to consider.

You could use:

> **Cardboard boxes**. They are inexpensive, and available in a wide range of shapes and sizes

> **Containers for suspension files**. These products are also available in several sizes and materials including both clear plastics and sturdy metals. They can fit nicely on a shelf, under a table or can even be stacked together

Rolling file cart. If you need to move a selection of your paperwork to different locations on a regular basis, you could use a rolling file cart

Multi mini drawer cabinet. Not everything you will be storing is paper thin. These cabinets have slightly deeper drawers that would be good for organising the more bulky supplies.

Stacking bins. Again, if you need to store products of an awkward shape, you could look at stacking bins

Kitchen cabinets. There seems to be a larger selection of wall kitchen cabinets than office specific cabinets. And since we are discussing storage containers and boxes there is no better time to tell you, "When it comes to storage you should think outside the box"

But don't forget there is still that old favourite:

The filing cabinet. This can be a great asset to your filing needs. After researching to find the best cabinet for a client I was pleased to see the amazing variety, colours and non-office looking designs there were. The cabinet that was purchased took up less space and held more paperwork than the tattered, mishmash of boxes the client was using previously

Make sure the system you do choose fits in your office, works best with your job and suits what you need to store.

The desk

This is where the majority of home workers will be spending their day. Even if you do not regularly work at a computer you will still be involved in various online activities like sending invoices, sorting accounts and e-mailing clients or customers. Or you will use the internet for marketing, research and networking

Albert Einstein asked, "If a cluttered desk signs a cluttered mind, then of what is an empty desk a sign?" To me this emphasises the importance of finding a happy medium and making sure your desk allows you to work at your best.

> **As they say in Monty Python's "Life of Brian" movie,**
> **"We are all individuals"**
> **and that is a wonderful thing.**

I have come across people who feel that being organised will stunt their creativity. My background is in fashion and design and the thought of creating a new outfit with piles of clutter and stuff around, quite frankly fills me with dread. That said, after an afternoon of creating there will be patterns, fabric and threads spread around the room, but once I've finished they are put away, ready for my next moment of creativity.

This is in line with the theme of this book, the fact that there is **no one perfect way** to organise and set up your desk. What you are aiming for is enough space to work effectively, have what you need close to hand, and not turn your desk into a dumping ground.

What do you need daily?

♦ Phone
♦ Computer
♦ Printer
♦ Computer paper
♦ Letter tray
♦ Pens, pencils
♦ Paperwork for current projects
♦ Client or customer information
♦ Industry specific equipment
♦ Waste bin

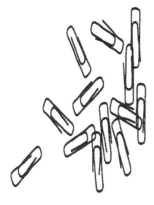

What is needed less frequently?

♦ Sticky tape
♦ Scissors
♦ Index pages
♦ Business card holder
♦ Stamps
♦ Binders
♦ Stapler
♦ Scanner and other computer gadgets
♦ A large portion of the paperwork
♦ Letterhead paper, envelopes

These lists can go on and on, so to make it easier check out the *checklists* section of the book.

The set up of your storage, filing and desk needs to be thought out as a group organisational package to allow a continual flow in the space. You want to think logically about the location of the storage containers and where each item will be stored.

To help with this flow, keep frequently used products within an arm's reach.

Ask yourself questions like:

➢ How often do you use the printer, is it necessary for it to be on the desk?

➢ Are there reference books you use daily, if not could they be stored on a high shelf?

➢ What tools are needed to keep you working efficiently and where is the sensible location for them to be stored?

➢ What set up is best for ease of use? Allow your thoughts to flow easily by allowing your hand to flow easily

As I mentioned earlier in the chapter, you need to streamline your paperwork which will leave an assortment to be archived. Look into the possibility of scanning the pages and saving them electronically, or store the items at the back of a shelf, high in a cupboard or in the less used location.

Remember the flow, and keep the convenient spaces free for items you use on a regular basis.

Personal paperwork

If your home office is also going to include personal paperwork and files, you will want to keep them stored separately. This can be accomplished by designating certain drawers to personal paperwork or a small filing container all on its own.

Keeping paperwork separate will also help you maintain your work/life balance, which I will be looking into in Chapter 7.

Back up on computer

With so much vital information being saved and stored on a computer, you must with a capital **M**, copy all your important files regularly. We are so reliant on computers that it would be a disaster if one day your computer broke. Do you think it would be possible for you to continue trading as a business if all the information suddenly disappeared?

You can back up by using:

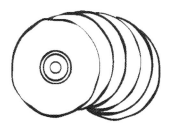

- ◆ USB memory stick
- ◆ CD-Rs
- ◆ DVD-Rs
- ◆ Online backup websites

There are several companies that offer back up services. I have listed a few in the *useful contacts* section of the book.

The lessons you have learned.

What are the first three action steps you will take to improve your storage?

1._____

_____

_____

_____

2._____

_____

_____

_____

3._____

_____

_____

_____

Chapter 4
Frame of Mind

Successfully working from home is so much more than sitting at your desk and starting to work. It is important to create what I call, your very own working from home **frame of mind**.

If you think about it, the environment does not drastically change. In one moment you are in your dressing gown having breakfast, and in the next you could be making business deals. This is why you need to create a working from home frame of mind and prevent the two areas of your life becoming muddled, resulting in dire consequences for both.

> There needs to be a trigger/routine to help shift your mindset from
> **home mode** to *work mode*.

What routine will help to trigger that shift? What routine will quickly allow you to be motivated, inspired, focused and ready to get on with a day of work? What routine will prepare you to get into a successful working from home **frame of mind?**

Think back to when you worked in an office building and the little routines that prepared you for your day. It may have been arriving at a train station, greeting the security guard or hanging your coat on the back of the chair. And of course, the important ritual of having your first cup of tea or coffee at the office.

But also be aware that not all the traditional office daily routines will suit a home office. They may not transfer perfectly, so pick the best or establish your own new routine.

I am always on a quest to learn as much as possible about how to work successfully from home, especially any new tips or techniques that are effective for those already working in this way. While at a conference I met Bruce. We had a long chat about his experiences of working from home and how initially he struggled with finding motivation in the morning. It had become such a problem that there was a discussion with his manager about the possibility of moving back to the office.

Things all changed when by a happy coincidence he decided to visit the gym before starting work. This gave his mornings a much needed routine and he returned back home full of energy and with the focus needed for the day ahead.

Bruce was able to find the trigger that let him easily shift into *work mode* and it is important that you find your trigger as well. That importance can increase when your week is split between being based at home and the office. This type of work schedule can introduce extra challenges. So you need to create a plan of action and put steps into place ensuring that you are able to work effectively in the different locations. Without realising it you already have a trigger when working at the office, but may need to introduce one for the days you are based at home.

In next chapter I will be looking into productive habits and how they can assist you in this process as well.

What routines can you add to your day that will allow you to get into the right frame of mind?

- Dress in office attire
- Only enter the office area when you are ready to work
- Spend a few minutes re-reading your goals
- Exercise
- Only eat breakfast in the kitchen never at your desk
- Walk the dog
- Have your morning coffee down at the local café
- Take ten minutes to meditate
- Start work only when the children have left for school
- Attend breakfast networking events

When you have your very own triggers that bring on an effective frame of mind, there is no time wasted. You will be able to start promptly, keep your focus and not be distracted by the various temptations in and around your home.

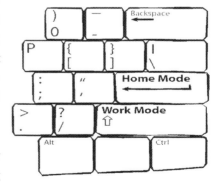

Throughout the next few chapters I will be looking at the skills, techniques, habits, and systems you need in order to work successfully from home. I also will be covering the tricky subject of time management and how to ensure your time is used more effectively.

The lessons you have learned.

What are the first three action steps you will take to establish your working from home *Frame of Mind*?

1._____

_____

_____

_____

2._____

_____

_____

_____

3._____

_____

_____

_____

Chapter 5
Productive Habits

There are certain habits you need in your working life to be more effective and productive, as well as habits that allow you to take advantage of the new working from home **frame of mind** you are establishing. You might find it surprising that I have chosen to use the word *habit* in the title of this chapter when I could have used words like skill, practice or routine.

> **The dictionary describes a habit as:**
>
> **An action or pattern of behaviour that is repeated so often that it becomes typical of somebody, although he or she may be unaware of it.**

The reason the word *habit* is best suited to this chapter is because as the dictionary says, you know a habit has been formed when you perform the action without even realising it. Wouldn't it be great to have plenty of positive habits that are a continual benefit to you?

Of course, introducing positive habits may take a commitment to establish them fully. Far too often bad habits seem to show up completely uninvited. But if you have the discipline to repeat the action until it becomes natural, you will be able to enjoy all the benefits of having established habits important to your success.

It is fair to say that you may need to learn a new style of working that suits being based at home. As mentioned in Chapter 4, not all of the habits or routines you developed while working in a traditional office will serve you best in this circumstance.

I mentioned in Chapter 2, that working from home can suit most people, especially if they have the determination to develop the skills necessary, so read on and be ready to develop new skills.

You have proven your determination just by reading this book. But what habits will serve you the best?

Various productive habits:

- ◆ Setting effective goals
- ◆ Preventing procrastination
- ◆ Setting boundaries
- ◆ Choosing powerful priorities
- ◆ Dealing with administration
- ◆ Establishing systems
- ◆ Creating a schedule
- ◆ Self organisation
- ◆ Self management
- ◆ Time management
- ◆ Setting useful routines

A number of these productive habits will be covered in the following chapters; however, right now we will look at setting goals.

Effective goals

How can you run a flourishing business or further your career if you do not know where you are going? To create effective goals, first establish what you want. There needs to be a very specific target that you are aiming for, otherwise it will be like drifting in a dinghy on a big empty ocean. You may eventually make it to where you were heading, but since it was such a roundabout route, you may have missed many opportunities along the way.

The same goes for carrying on with your business life without goals.

You have great plans for the business. There are new clients to obtain, higher turnover to achieve, and an organised office to create; but for this to happen you need to choose the goals that will help you get there.

What do you want?

- ♦ Look at all that you aspire to accomplish in the next week, month, year
- ♦ What is most important to you?
- ♦ What will help to develop your career?
- ♦ Do you need expert help to expand your business?
- ♦ What will improve the balance in your life?
- ♦ Where do you want your business to go?
- ♦ What will need to happen to make you a success?
- ♦ Do you need further training to gain a promotion?

Once you have decided what you want, there are certain proven steps you need to take when setting goals.

Already Achieved

Start to visualise and imagine that you have already achieved your goal. How do you feel and what does achieving your goal look like? How are colleagues, manager and associates treating you? What does having success sound like? You want to create a sharp vision so that it feels like you have already accomplished the goal and can see it in **High Definition** with bright colours and surround sound.

Specific

Be specific. Your goal should not be, "I want more clients". It needs to be, "I will have 10 new clients by the 29th of September (5 months away) this year". Each goal needs to be written as a

positive statement and describe what needs to happen in order for you to achieve the goal. This includes who, what, when, where, which, and why.

Measurable

It is important to track your progress along the way, and make any changes necessary so that the goal is reached. The goal of 10 additional clients by September will mean on average two new clients a month. If you have achieved three new clients in three months, it would be a good idea to re-evaluate your goal and revisit whether it is attainable, as we will be looking at next.

Attainable

This section is all about planning the steps necessary to ensure your goal becomes a reality. To achieve the goal, do you need to improve your skills, attitude or abilities in any way? Do you need to go on a marketing course? Are there any resources you could look into? Should you ask for help from other experts? A sign of strength is knowing your limitations while at the same time striving to learn more, expand your mind and seek new possibilities.

Make use of all available opportunities to attain your goal.

Realistic

A common mistake is setting unrealistic goals. Again looking at our goal of 10 new clients, imagine that you have decided it will be 200 new clients instead. Is that realistic? Where will they be found? Are you setting yourself up for disappointment and new frustrations? Look at how many clients you obtained in the past year and use that information to help set a more realistic goal.

If the goal is not realistic, the whole process will only have a negative effect on what you want to accomplish.

Timed

Your goal requires an overall start and finish date, but each action step also needs a specific competition date. If dates are not included, you will just keep on working towards something but never know when you have arrived. How frustrating would that be. It would rob you of great success and enjoyment of what you have achieved.

There are a few more important tips for successful goals:

> ➢ Set short and long term goals or a combination of both. Any large (long term) goal will need smaller (short term) goals to be achieved along the way for the final goal to be reached

> ➢ If you have set several goals, you need to prioritise each one according to how important they are and which steps or tasks you will be carrying out first. I look at priorities further in Chapter 6. Being able to prioritise will help to avoid that feeling of being overwhelmed, frustrated and eventually giving up all together

> ➢ Evaluate your progress on a regular basis and make any adjustments necessary

> ➢ Have your goals written down and place the goals in a location where you can view them regularly

> ➢ Note down the tasks you have decided to carry out, in your diary or electronic organiser

> ➢ Tell a supportive and positive friend or mentor your goals. Being accountable to someone else could be the extra motivation you need when you have lost your focus

> ➢ Celebrate when you achieve a goal

Administration

This chapter is covering **productive home working habits,** and nothing will have a greater effect on your productivity than ensuring that the administration side of your office is organised. This is a big subject and one that could have a book written about it all on its own. But for now I am focusing on *understanding your organising approach*, effectively dealing with *filing and paperwork,* and *systems and processes* to implement.

In Chapter 3 I looked at office storage and streamlining your paperwork to get it under control. Now to go one step further I will cover the subject of office administration and how to make sure it works best for you.

You may have had experience of working in a traditional office where you were only responsible for your department within the company, because there were:

- ◆ Personal assistants
- ◆ Accountants
- ◆ A marketing department
- ◆ IT experts
- ◆ A sales department

Many entrepreneurs decide to start their own business and work from home so that they can do what they love. However, with that can come responsibility for the unexciting activities because there isn't the backup support, and having the administration area up to scratch will make this easier.

Your organising approach

We all have our own way of thinking and sorting information in our heads. This is another example of how there is *no one perfect way of working from home*. You want to establish habits that will drastically increase your productivity and efficiency, and reduce the stress brought on by clutter and lost paperwork. Having an understanding of your organising approach and finding your own administration procedures will help to accomplish this.

> **Wandering:** Does your mind wander regularly because of being preoccupied with all the other work still to be completed? Do you work on several tasks at once, but never fully focus on anything? This is a disastrous waste of time especially when you jump from one task to another.
>
> You need to introduce procedures that will increase your focus. One tip would be to schedule the challenging tasks during your peak concentration times of the day.

> **Visual:** This is when information needs to be in view and not tucked away in a file, computer or under a pile of clutter.
>
> It was a revelation for Millie who realised that no matter how the filing system was set up, if her urgent paperwork was not on the desk she just could not remember it existed. The procedure we put in place was to introduce a single in-tray on the desk where important work was to be placed. Once completed, it then could be filed .

➤ **Perfectionist**: This is a demanding approach to uphold. It requires you to maintain unrealistic standards that can take up too much of your time. You thrive in the details and can expend all your energy making sure everything is perfect, but not always achieving what you need to.

I recommend introducing a more realistic approach. It is unwise to suffocate under the expectation of perfection as everyone has a different view and opinion of how well any task has been completed.

➤ **Indecisive**: Not sure what to do next, how to start, or where to file anything. Indecision can destroy any dreams of becoming organised. Sarah was extremely indecisive, she worried all the time about whether or not an item was

 in the correct place or, if something had been thrown out, whether or not it would be missed. When I first met Sarah, she was unable to make the simplest of decisions, resulting in a cluttered life. Fortunately, she was open to change and is now enjoying an organised office gained through learning how to be confident with her decisions.

One organising tip that works well for the indecisive is to keep your filing categories fairly broad. Think large sections, not hundreds of little categories.

> **Piler**: You are not a fan of the filing cabinet; it all seems too fiddly and fussy. About three seconds into the first consultation with Katie it became apparent that she was definitely not a fan of her filing cabinet. In fact she had hit it with a cricket bat one frustrated afternoon.

> For Katie the solution was to use several box files that were divided into broad sections, and for quick access they were stored on a shelving unit.

> **Filer**: You crave structured procedures and systems, and the filing cabinet is your favourite organising tool.

With every organising approach there are strengths and weaknesses. The aim is to use the strengths and find procedures that will help to look after the administrative side of the office.

Filing and paperwork

There is so much information to cover in this section that I have decided to use bullet points in order to get the information across as quickly as possible. Also, to keep it simple, I will be sticking to the word **filing** to describe the general process even if it is not your preferred style.

Remember in Chapter 3 I covered the significance of sorting, de-cluttering, and streamlining your paperwork. This is an important administration routine and one that needs to be repeated regularly to keep your paperwork under control.

Now you need to establish your **filing system.** Make sure the system is not too complicated or intricate, keep it simple so that any-one can step in and deal with the filing after receiving only minimal instructions. If it becomes any more complicated than that, even you may forget what the system is and chaos will follow.

Guidelines to organising files:

➢ De-clutter. When you are establishing your filing, it is best not to waste space on paperwork not needed

➢ Decide on organising supplies and equipment

➢ Label

➢ Sort alphabetically, by category or numerically

➢ Decide if you are going to put recent information in the front of a file or at the back and stick to that system

➢ Keep the sections broad and don't get distracted by making a category for every little piece of paperwork

➢ Keep personal and business files separate

➢ Put the effort into creating a well organised filing system that you will use

➢ Leave room for expansion

➢ File and streamline regularly

There is no denying that administration and paperwork are not exciting for many people. Even I can admit that I am not a huge fan of filing. Do you remember how it was predicted that we would all be getting around in flying cars by now? Well, that seems to be similar to the idea of a paperless office, still very far off in the future.

Here are some ideas to help you deal with the paperwork:

- Set a specific time to file
- File regularly, remember the little and often rule
- Sort the post as soon as it arrives
- Be ruthless
- Establish a temporary holding system for paperwork that needs to be actioned before getting filed
- Decide straight away where the item will go
- Sort paperwork near shredder, bin and recycle box
- Recycle
- Shred papers with any personal information
- Cancel all magazine/industry subscriptions
- Request to be removed from junk mail lists
- Keep paperwork electronically whenever possible
- Don't print out anything unnecessarily
- Hire in office help to do the filing

What to keep?

- All account information
- Irreplaceable information
- Paperwork kept for legal reasons
- Current or previous project paperwork
- Current client information and inquiries
- Personal information, passport, birth certificates, wills
- Business insurance

What not to keep?

- Anything with no specific purpose or 'just in case'

Next we look at the desk, which is not only a magnet for clutter and paperwork but also for used coffee cups. Earlier I brought your attention to Albert Einstein's thoughts on what a cluttered desk is a sign of. But when it comes to the desk area, you want to make sure it allows you to work at your best.

The desk:

- Not a dumping ground
- Only stores the paperwork you are using today
- Not a location for personal trinkets
- Should be cleared at the end of the day
- Not a place to store any non-office related items
- Should allow you to complete your work with ease
- Should not be the cause of stress

Systems

The next key element in organising the administration side of your office is by establishing systems. You want the systems to become a habit that will allow you to simply and easily deal with repetitive tasks without much fuss.

Let us look at a situation where having a system in place would be beneficial. You met an individual whilst networking who has shown particular interest in what you do and briefly mentioned that they would like to speak to you again. Now you are back in the office, what should you do? You need a system to record their details and a system that will allow you to keep in regular contact with the individual.

It would be wise to follow up this contact because on average it takes over seven interactions before potential customers will make a purchase or use your service.

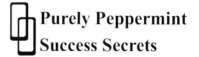 **Purely Peppermint Success Secrets**

Depending on your organising style, you can either:
clear your desk at the end of the day and start fresh the next day;
Or
when rejuvenated in the morning clear the desk and start off with setting your goals for the day.

When you have systems in place to deal with your regular work, activities or tasks it creates a highly productive environment.

You need a system for:

- ♦ Client enquiries
- ♦ Invoices
- ♦ Late payments
- ♦ Database updating
- ♦ Estimates, Quotations
- ♦ Tendering
- ♦ Handling sales orders
- ♦ All book keeping and accounts
- ♦ Answering emails
- ♦ Booking appointments
- ♦ Payroll
- ♦ Checking orders before dispatch
- ♦ Any paperwork used regularly
- ♦ Project planning
- ♦ Handling returns or complaints

How you sort and deal with the administration side of an office can make or break you. Tyler called me in desperation because his out of control paperwork was effecting his reputation and had just lost him a lucrative client. We spent three days clearing the office of everything not needed before even being able to set up a filing system that best suited his administration style. Now he is more in control.

The lessons you have learned.

What are the first three action steps you will take to establish the productive habits you need?

1._____

_____

_____

_____

2._____

_____

_____

_____

3._____

_____

_____

_____

Chapter 6
Managing your Time

Being able to master your time while based at home can be a tricky thing. Actually, time management can be tricky no matter where you work. This is why I prefer to call it *self management* and how you manage your time, rather than the more commonly used term of *time management* and how time manages you.

Time moves on and no matter what you do, there will still only be 24 hours in a day. But how you manage your time will determine how much you accomplish in those 24 hours.

So far I have already covered a few habits that will help to improve your self management:

> A professionally set up office will have a positive effect on your time, because it allows you to work at your best

> An organised storage system will save you time because you can find what you need quickly and easily

> Finding your **working from home** *frame of mind* allows you to focus completely on work and let the thoughts about home leak away until later

> Setting effective goals will have a positive motivational effect and give you the drive to complete the tasks needed to accomplish your goals

To help you manage your time even better, I will be sharing more of my success secrets.

Schedule

The first step to self management is developing a schedule. Nothing wastes time like staring off into space not knowing what to do next. Remember **prior planning and perfect preparation prevents poor performance**, and it also prevents time from slipping away.

There are different ways you can keep track of your schedule. If electronic gadgets keep you organised, then choose one of the many Personal Digital Assistants (PDA) on the market. Most new

 mobile phones have calendars with alarms where you can create your schedule. If your day is spent out of the office, make use of a *Smartphone* where you can surf the net and receive your emails. Or if you prefer your information to be written down a Filofax type paper diary may be more to your liking. For the home workers based at home full time a computer calendar can keep track of everything on your schedule and send you regular reminders.

What you use to keep track of your schedule isn't as important as the fact that you have created a schedule in the first place.

For the Personal Digital Assistant, Diary or Calendar to be of any use you need to **schedule everything important:**

- ♦ Current projects
- ♦ Business meetings, deadlines, appointments
- ♦ Marketing
- ♦ Accounting
- ♦ Clients to contact
- ♦ Filing
- ♦ Networking
- ♦ Holidays
- ♦ All tasks and assignments
- ♦ Daytime family responsibilities

Your schedule will incorporate both short and long term items. Start by scheduling the long term tasks including everything that needs to take place for the task to be completed. Then slot in the short term tasks, either on a daily basis or as they arrive. Having flexibility and being able to make adjustment when it is needed, are fundamental to a successful schedule.

This is when you need to be the master of your time.

Are there non-vital items for the day that could be removed? Do you need to change the schedule in order to fit in a specific task for a newly assigned project? What do you need to do today?

Being able to prioritise the tasks in your schedule is vital and I will be taking a closer look at that next.

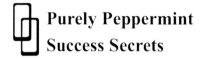

Purely Peppermint Success Secrets

Any schedule needs to include that little bit of extra time
to give you the flexibility for when things do not go quite to plan.

Do not schedule everything back to back and make sure there is **extra time** in your schedule.

Priorities

So far you have established your filing system, been developing productive habits, setting up systems, schedules and routines. All of this will be beneficial in helping with how you manage your time. But do you still find there are days when there never seems to be enough time to complete everything? And even if you do complete all the tasks you have scheduled, it seems as if your business or career is not moving forward.

It's possible that you have been choosing the wrong project, task or assignment to work on. Are you selecting the first thing that comes to mind or are you choosing work that will have the greatest outcome to your business or career? In other words are you prioritising your tasks?

If not, here is some advice on how to start prioritising.

Learning the skill of prioritising will lead to the most astonishing improvement on how your time is managed. While working with Sean, it became obvious that he was caught in the habit of dealing with the easy tasks before the important and essential ones. Sean thought he was accomplishing so much as he marked tasks off his "to do" list , but was mistaking action for progress.

To decide what priority should be given to any item, **there are a few questions you want to ask**?

- ◆ Is this urgent?
- ◆ Is this vital?
- ◆ Is it important?
- ◆ Does this move you towards your goal?
- ◆ What will happen if you never carry out this task?
- ◆ Are you doing this task to avoid doing something else?
- ◆ Will this further your career?
- ◆ Will this have a positive impact on your business?
- ◆ Is this the best use of your time?
- ◆ What will be achieved when this task is completed?
- ◆ What one thing do you want to accomplish today?

The answers to these questions will help you to prioritise tasks that are a benefit to your business or career and the best use of your time.

Do you only work on the urgent tasks and feel that you are never on top of your work? You need to prioritise what is important over what you think is urgent. Let's look into that a bit more.

Urgent or Important tasks

What is the difference between urgent and important tasks and how do you use this difference in creating an effective schedule? Urgent tasks are the ones that put you into panic mode. Because when you haven't been prioritising tasks correctly the deadline closes in, panic begins, and the tasks becomes **urgent.**

Important tasks are the ones that help you to progress towards your goals, further your career or develop your business. What you want to be is proactive in creating your schedule. By doing this, you will avoid the panic of reacting to events when they have become **urgent** by having dealt with them when they were just **important**.

Important	Urgent
Choose these tasks first. That way you will avoid the panic and resulting stress because you didn't prioritise correctly and now the situation has turned urgent.	Do not choose what is urgent, but focus on what is **Important.**

I taught Sean the benefits of prioritising tasks important to his business. When we looked at his previous choices, it revealed many holes in his decision making skills. Now, the first thing he asks when going through the schedule or deciding what to prioritise is, "What important task should I work on today that will be a benefit to my business and ensure that I reach my goals?" You can ask yourself the same.

Routine

Right alongside scheduling your specific work and tasks for the day, sits scheduling a daily routine.

What tasks happen every day that will allow you to deliver your product or service?

Unlike being based in a traditional office building you now have the opportunity to set a routine that will suit your needs. Draw upon your previous work experiences and transfer any of the successful structures you used there into your new routine.

Don't let being based at home trick you subconsciously into becoming unprofessional. If you are just winging it rather than creating a routine, subconsciously you may not be taking work seriously and this could translate into low results. By establishing a routine, let's say working 9am-5pm Monday-Friday it will help with your working from home **frame of mind** and give you a structure for the essential shift into *work mode*.

Routines you should include:

- Start time
- Finish time
- Lunch time
- Frame of mind trigger
- Days off
- Anything that occurs regularly

When you routinely work the same hours and days of the week it assists in allowing family members or individuals sharing your environment to become accustomed to your schedule. Through this familiarity, and setting boundaries (which we will look at a bit later), you will be allowed the space and freedom needed to work effectively.

Do not underestimate the benefit of regular breaks, they help to keep you fresh and focused.

Peak time

In every job there are certain tasks that are more mundane and challenging than others. For your schedule to be as effective as possible, you will need to identify what your **peak times of the day** are.

> ➤ Are you a morning person bursting with energy and full of gusto early in the day, only to lose your motivation just after lunch?

> ➤ Are you an evening person and your day gets off to a slow start only for a burst of energy to appear later in the afternoon until late in the night?

Only you will know when your energy is abundant and with that information you can schedule challenging tasks during a time when you feel fresh and focused. This leaves the easier tasks for when you are lethargic and low in motivation.

Say No

Are you a people pleaser? Do you take on every piece of work, no matter what it is or no matter how much time you have free?

Can you say, "No!"?

When you have your own business, it seems almost impossible to say no. When you are a home based employee you may feel as if you need to take on *everything* just to please your boss and convince them that you are *really* working.

If you are not able to set boundaries and **say no**, you could end up burning yourself out. **Have the confidence to decline anything that is not a high priority or important**. When there is an imminent deadline, let the phone go to voice mail, turn off your e-mail and focus on the task on which you are currently working.

It is ok to say no to:

- Any invitation that will interrupt your day
- Callers to your door
- Unrealistic expectations you have about yourself
- Interrupting emails
- Networking events
- Unnecessary meetings
- Interrupting phone calls
- Unnecessary work

There will be requests very specific to you that require a confident refusal.

Customers will understand that you are busy, much more than they will welcome a missed deadline. How you refuse is all down to your expertise. It doesn't always have to be an abrupt "No!". It could be something along the line of, "I am fully booked right now, but am able to fit you in on such and such a date" or simply, "I am free on this date".

So much better than this well known situation.......

This is certainly not a representation of the whole industry, but have you ever had this experience when you hire a builder? At the beginning they are around all the time busily getting on with

the work. All of a sudden they disappear; you can't seem to get a hold of them, resulting in your home being completed weeks or even months late. What do you think of the company now? Would you ever refer them onto a friend? Or, would you have preferred a realistic deadline that was met?

This is an important lesson to learn. Being reliable and true to your word is an important "value" for you and/or your business to encompass.

Keep focused on tasks

Jumping from one task to another without actually completing anything is obviously very unproductive. What you need is the ability to focus on one item at a time. In this chapter so far you have created a schedule and established a regular routine, but there are still a few more items needed to make sure you will be fully focused.

Eliminate distraction

When working from home your focus can be tempted away and distracted at every turn. What are you being distracted by? It takes extra discipline to work at home and by eliminating distraction you will create an environment where there is the space for you to focus.

What is distracting you?	What can you do?
Uninvited salespeople.	Leave the door unanswered.
Email Notifications.	Only respond to emails at certain times of the day.
Friends who drop by.	Politely let them know you are busy.
Phone calls.	Let the calls go to voice mail or let the answering machine take the call.
Household chores.	Ignore them during office hours.

In the next chapter I will be investigating ways to resolve any of the sensitive issues regarding family and friends interrupting your day.

Outsource

As you know you cannot do everything and being based at home sometimes requires you to take care of tasks that are not always part of your specific area of expertise. Understanding the power of outsourcing and not micromanaging every single task is the sign of a successful individual.

You could outsource to a:

- Virtual Assistant
- Accountant
- IT support service
- PR company
- Office helper for the filing and paperwork
- Event organiser
- Marketing Company
- Data inputer
- Web designer

When you outsource any of the extra activities, it will free you up to focus on the tasks that generate more money.

The lessons you have learned.

What are the first three action steps you will take to improve how you manage your time?

1._____

_____

_____

_____

2._____

_____

_____

_____

3._____

_____

_____

_____

Chapter 7
Finding that Balance

Not only is redressing the **work/life balance** in your life one of the top reasons why individuals choose to work from home, but it is also one of the greatest benefits.

When your office is only one door away, you could turn into a workaholic and your **work life** could end up not leaving any space for your **home life**.

Is your life a little out of balance?

If so, think back to the reasons why you originally chose to work from home. Was it to reduce business start-up costs, to bring greater flexibility into your life, or to reduce stress? Whatever the reason was, I am sure it was not to end up working 24/7.

Before we move onto looking at ways of bringing your life back onto an even keel, you need to explore the current state of your work/life balance.

- How balanced are you?
- Is your work life taking over your home life?
- Are you too distracted by your home life to put in a full day's work?
- Are financial issues forcing you to work long hours?

Throughout this book I have covered several subjects that will restore your balance and ensure you are enjoying all the benefits that working from home can bring.

➢ In Chapters 2 and 3 we looked at setting up the office area and storage solutions. When you have a designated office space designed specifically to your needs it enables you to form a separation between **home** and **work life**

➢ In Chapter 4 we looked at establishing a *Working from Home Frame of Mind*. Make sure to create your frame of mind routines so that your **work life** does not end up taking over

➢ In Chapter 5 we covered many key factors for a healthy balance; each and every one could be included in this chapter as well. But if I had to highlight the top two, they would be **setting goals** and **establishing systems**

➢ Setting goals will keep you on track and being on track will give you focus

➢ Establishing systems will provide a balancing frame-work that will allow you to deal simply and quickly with all the regular office administration activities

➢ Managing both your *time* and *work/life* balance are very closely linked. In Chapter 6 we looked at managing your time and creating a schedule, but your schedule needs further investigation with regards to work /life balance.

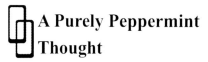

A Purely Peppermint Thought

Your understanding and interpretation of balance may be different from what it means to your manager, business partner or spouse.

To keep peace and balance in your working environment, it may be necessary to clarify the balance you are aiming for.

Your work/life balance schedule needs to include:

♦ Definite working hours
♦ Days off
♦ Annual holidays
♦ Time with the family
♦ Time with friends
♦ Time away from the office

It is a false economy to think that working nonstop is effective when the opposite is true. You need to schedule time for the people and activities you love and prevent the balance from tipping too far to one side.

Remembering **saying no**, is another important area for your balance. We looked at it from a *time management* point of view in Chapter 6. But from a work/life balance point of view, it is imperative to 'say no' to any activity, commitment or request that will have a negative consequence and upset your balance.

Family business meeting

I always recommend that clients consider holding a family business meeting. Having good communication skills is a valuable home working trait, and now is the time to put those skills to use.

Round up everyone who lives in the property (age appropriate) and gather at the dining room table. This is a meeting where each individual should have their say.

Get everything out in the open:

- ♦ Agree your working hours
- ♦ Agree on when is best for you to be interrupted
- ♦ Agree on how you would like to be interrupted
- ♦ Find out whether there are any apprehensions
- ♦ Talk about any potential problems
- ♦ Be willing to compromise

If any issues become apparent, use this opportunity to find a suitable solution. When the family is on board, it will help with a smooth running home office and keep you balanced and on track.

Get away from your desk

Always take your lunch and tea breaks away from the desk or even better, head outside where the fresh air will re-energise you.

Socialise

Are there friends you haven't seen for ages? Are there special events you want to attend, or do you need to bring the balance back into your family time together? Now that you are scheduling time off, you have an opportunity to get out there and start enjoying life. Ensure there are days which are for anything but work and remember to shut the office door at the end of the day.

Exercise

If you are sitting at a desk all day you might not be in the best shape of your life. Exercise or movement of some kind needs to be a regular part of your day. It doesn't always have to be as formal as the gym or joining a sports team, if that doesn't appeal to you. So be creative and get active.

Exercise is not only good for your *work/ life balance*, it is also good for every aspect of your life.

The lessons you have learned.

What are the first three action steps you will take in order to bring balance into your life?

1._____

_____

_____

_____

2._____

_____

_____

_____

3._____

_____

_____

_____

Chapter 8
Managing Isolation

For some people, staring at the same four walls everyday can drive them a little stir-crazy. Some of the qualities needed to increase your success when working from home were covered in Chapter 1. Now we will look at some additional qualities that will allow you to deal with potential periods of isolation.

The most successful home workers have developed the following behaviours and attitudes:

- ♦ Capable of working well on your own
- ♦ Self motivated
- ♦ Comfortable with the feelings of isolation
- ♦ Self reliant
- ♦ Confident in your abilities
- ♦ Aware of your limitations
- ♦ Self management skills
- ♦ A willingness to learn

Even if you have all of these qualities and thrive when working on your own, there will still be occasions when you require the company of others to stay healthy, intellectually stimulated and motivated.

It can be lonely working from home.

> ➢ There isn't the opportunity to have a good face to face catch up regarding the previous evening's TV shows, sports event or a general gossip session with colleagues during a tea break

> ➢ You may feel you are losing track of relationships with colleagues who were once part of your team back in the days when you were based at the office

> ➢ If a problem arises, chances are you don't have an expert on site who can fix it, so now it's your responsibility to find a solution and establish your own support team

> ➢ There isn't anyone sitting at the next desk who can look over your business ideas, give inspiration, or simply re-spond to a quick question

> ➢ When you are feeling frustrated and need to get an issue off your chest, there isn't a sympathetic colleague around to have lunch with

> ➢ While everyone else is going to the pub after a full day at the office you are home alone with the cat

As I re-read the previous points it seems to be so very negative and almost sounds as though when it comes to isolation, work-ing from home is the worst idea ever. This is not the case and happily all of the issues I raised are simple to solve.

Even if one of the reasons you decided to be based at home was for peace and quiet (i.e. a bit more isolation), and to provide the opportunity to increase your productivity without interruptions, there is no reason to let the feelings of isolation overwhelm you.

Things to remember.

Do keep in regular touch with business contacts, colleagues and associates

Do not think you are capable of doing everything yourself

Do remember you need other people and should get out of the house every day

Do not interact only online (facebook, twitter, e-mail)

Do keep in regular contact with your friends and family, which in Chapter 7 you already scheduled. This will prevent you from being engulfed in a **working from home bubble**

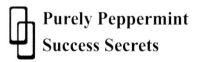

Purely Peppermint Success Secrets

When working in an office, communication with colleagues can happen naturally.
Now based at home, it will take conscious effort to remain in touch.

There are several ways to remain connected with the world and I will go through some online and offline ideas to create the interaction and connections you need.

Online

Home working organisations
These days there are quite a few organisations that focus on home based business owners and employees. They have the facility to pose questions, offer business solutions, find business connections, and give you a chance to talk with people who will understand your situation.

Networking groups
Belonging to an online networking group keeps you in touch with business owners of all types including both home and office workers. You will find contact details for home working and networking groups in the *Useful Contacts* section of the book. But take

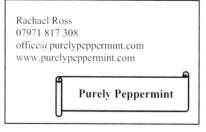

Rachael Ross
07971 817 308
office@purelypeppermint.com
www.purelypeppermint.com

Purely Peppermint

care that you don't end up spending too much time online, so keep to a time limit.

Blogs and Twitter
Take advantage of new communication tools by joining *Twitter* or writing a **Blog**. They are great for getting your name out there, promoting a business or product, and meeting new and interesting people.

Phone

Don't forget the old fashioned communications tools as well. To find an answer quickly there is nothing quite like using the phone.

Recently I was working with Phil, a client of mine who always insisted on e-mailing me several questions throughout the day. The messages arrived one right after the other, and one often coming in before I had had a chance to answer the previous one. It was not a good use of our time especially when one simple phone call would have been enough to answer all his questions. People appreciate the personal touch and a phone call will reduce any potential misunderstandings. It certainly did for my dealings with Phil.

Technology

As well as the phone, make use of the various communications technologies available. There are text/SMS, Skype and instant messaging to mention a few. The wider a variety of technology you embrace, the greater your personal connections will be and isolation will seem like a distant memory.

Offline face to face communication

Spending all day online hiding behind a computer may increase your feelings of isolation. It is your responsibility to get out there and have human contact.

Not only will face to face contact help fight a feeling of isolation and loneliness, it is also known to reduce stress levels.

For the self employed and business owner you can keep in touch face to face and promote your business by:

Meeting up

If you are planning on seeing a colleague, potential client or a mentor, then meet up in the nice relaxed atmosphere of a café. I have a favourite café which has become my *Café Office*, where I go to for a change of view, and to get re-energised. For a café meeting, make sure to prepare what you need ahead of time and have everything with you, e.g. brochures, product samples or your laptop. Running back to your office when you have forgotten something will not look professional.

For complete privacy and a traditional office environment you can hire meeting rooms at conference venues, business centres and in hotels.

Joining a mastermind group

I belong to a mastermind group, where six entrepreneurs meet every month to discuss a specific issue over which one of the members is currently pondering. We all offer our advice, experience and potential solutions to their troubling issue.

Sometimes when based at home it may feel as though you need to be the master of everything, which is unrealistic. Having access to a mastermind group is a great way for me to establish a support system of other experts ready and willing to help. If there isn't already a local group, start one of your own. I can't recommend it enough.

Join a networking group

As well as online networking, you should be getting involved with the local networking organisations as they are also a great place to find help and support. Research the various groups in your area and select a group that will meet your business needs.

There is a wide assortment of groups with an equally wide range of joining costs. Some groups only allow one member in each profession, giving you the opportunity to establish yourself as the local expert.

Getting exercise

Exercise is important enough to have been mentioned twice. Nothing beats isolation like leaving your home office and power walking during lunchtime with a neighbour or taking part in a dance class with a friend.

Employees can keep in touch by:

Even if you are a home based employee you will need to have face to face communication. This is helpful in maintaining the connections and relationships you have with colleagues you don't see everyday.

Trade and industry associations

If you want to stay current, meet likeminded individuals and make sure your face is being seen by the right people, you will want to join any associations relevant to your industry. There can be plenty of networking at these events and you never know what profitable connections you may make.

Attend socials

Let your employees and colleagues know that you are still a vital part of the team by attending any company socials. This will give you the opportunity to increase your rapport with team members, meet new employees and have some fun.

It is unfortunate that home based employees are still perceived in a slightly negative way by some office based colleagues. One reservation could be that colleagues don't fully understand how productive working from home is for each individual and the business as a whole. Attending work socials is an opportunity to bond and make connections with colleagues that can reduce these misunderstandings.

The lessons you have learned.

What are the first three action steps you will take in order to create the interaction and connections you need?

1._____

_____

_____

_____

2._____

_____

_____

_____

3._____

_____

_____

_____

Chapter 9
Bring it all Together

So, now you have read the book, hopefully jotted down a few ideas and enjoyed learning new behaviours and attitudes that will help you become even more successful when working from home. The lessons you have learned are now buzzing with inspiration and positive energy to take you into the future. But now what?

To get the most from this book, make a plan and implement it immediately. Refer back to that plan when you need to.

> ➢ Follow through with the action steps you selected

> ➢ Decide what to improve in your office area

> ➢ Decide what productive habits you can introduce

> ➢ Decide which changes you need to make happen

> ➢ Take action now

> ➢ Re-read this book in six weeks time to remind you of how best to work from home

**Successfully working from home is now in your hands
Take the steps needed to create your very own perfect
way of working from home.**

The lessons you have learned.

What are the first three action steps you are going to take in order to make working from home a success for you?

1._____

_____

_____

_____

2._____

_____

_____

_____

3._____

_____

_____

_____

Bonus Chapter
Money Saving Organising Tips

Times are becoming tougher, sales are down on last year, money is tight and banks are not lending. One of the reasons you may have chosen to work from home was to reduce your outlay and expenses.

The costs are lower because:

- No separate office building
- Lower start up outlay
- No child care costs
- No commuting costs for the train/bus tickets or running a car

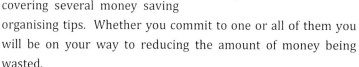

You have been enjoying those savings for a couple of years, but now what. As businesses are feeling the squeeze are there any other ways you can reduce your expenses?

In this bonus chapter I am covering several money saving organising tips. Whether you commit to one or all of them you will be on your way to reducing the amount of money being wasted.

De-clutter

In Chapter 3 we discussed clearing and de-cluttering your office. This is a significant money saving tip so it is mentioned again in this chapter. When your office is full of clutter it has such a negative effect on your productivity, and the less productive you are the lower your earnings will be. But still many seem to underestimate the importance of this simple activity. Instead you wade through all the paperwork and other household clutter expelling a needless amount of extra time searching for what you need.

That time would be better spent on extra work, new projects, or marketing and meeting new clients. All of which could increase your turnover and bring in more money.

Take action

Not taking action is a destroyer of success. When you take little steps you are continually moving forward, but when you do nothing, nothing happens, nothing improves and nothing progresses. At the end of every chapter you had the opportunity to decide what actions you were going to take and if you have been debating for days on end whether you should do this or do that, choose what seems or feels best at the moment and start there.

Take action to get organised. Know what you have, so you don't buy another just because you couldn't find the one you already had.

Be aware of how you use your time

One definition of madness is "doing the same thing over and over again and expecting a different result". Now is not the time to be complacent, but rather to become aware of the activities that waste valuable time and money.

- ♦ What makes those activities so wasteful?
- ♦ Why do you continually choose to do them?
- ♦ What are you doing that is slightly mad?

Be adaptable

Once you have awareness you next need to be adaptable. If you are using the self-destructive excuse of saying, "Well that is just the way we have always done it" you will end up suffering unnecessary negative consequences. Look at your activities, tasks and priorities and ask yourself:

"Where do I need to adapt and do something different?"

Have a flexible approach

Maintain a flexible attitude in your business dealings. You need to be able to make quick adjustments and ensure the satisfaction of your clients, customers or manager to increase sales and productivity.

Prepare and have a professional image

Whenever there is an important meeting the following morning, I spend the final few minutes of my time in the office preparing

properly for it. I make sure I have all my usual supplies, plus any additional products or materials that might be needed such as catalogues, brochures, etc.

It does amaze me when I meet a fellow business owner at a networking event and they are without their business cards. If an individual is asking for your contact details, chances are they are interested in your business and one day may lead onto becoming a customer. When you don't have a basic marketing tool like your business cards it will not show you or your business in the best possible light. This will make you look disorganised, unreliable and give the impression that you may offer a substandard service or product.

Would you hire a business like that?

Prepare what you need for any business situations. We live in a world of snap judgment and decisions, so show that you are an organised and efficient individual determined to beat off the competition.

Make smart purchases

In Chapter 2 we talked about one of Purely Peppermint's success secrets regarding the fact that buying every piece of organising equipment and storage container will not make you organised and wastes money.

You need to decide what your filing, storage and office requirements are before you purchase anything, so that you can buy wisely.

Now is the time to use that wisdom and purchase only:

- ♦ What you need
- ♦ What will increase your profits
- ♦ What will increase your productivity
- ♦ What brings you real joy
- ♦ What is vital to your success

Self control

A lack of self control and succumbing to impulse purchases is a recurring theme with many of my clients. I regularly find multiple quantities of the same item during the process of working together to clear their clutter and establish order.

Again as with smart buying, only buy what you need and if you feel an impulse purchase approaching, use self control and commit to making only *smart purchases.*

Group activities

I have already advised you to establish a routine and schedule your activities; this tip will be expanding on that advice.

To make smart use of your time, schedule all similar tasks simultaneously. Just imagine if you had to venture out to the bank, the accountant, buy supplies and see one client. Why not group the activities together and take care of them in one trip? The same can be said for any office tasks. To avoid interrupting your routine and thus reducing productivity, group together activities like responding to e-mails, taking care of the filing, or making phone calls.

Organise personal receipts

Keep your receipts (with guarantees and instruction manuals) in a file that you will be able to locate quickly. That way if you ever need to return anything broken or unwanted you can do so because you have proof of purchase.

Organise business accounts

Make sure to have your business accounts and receipts organised. This is a vital part of working from home that requires the effective system you established after reading Chapter 5. With the economy struggling you need to know exactly how much money you have, where it is coming from and where it is going.

Organise your client's payments

It is important in business to decide how you are going to deal with customers or clients who consistently pay late. This might not have been a problem in the past but times have changed and we are in a new financial environment, so be prepared by having procedures in place.

- How much leeway is going to be allowed?
- Will you call in an external debt collector if needed?
- What changes can you make to your current terms and conditions that will reduce late payments?

It will be far easier to deal with any late payments when your business accounts are organised and you have all the systems in place.

Automate your payments

To save money, you need to set up automatic payments for anything that needs to be paid regularly and avoid late charges or interest.

Also, some companies are offering a small discount if you receive your bills online rather than through the post.

Money saving frame of mind

This is going to be your *money saving frame of mind.* In tough times we have a tendency to focus on the negative when there are plenty of positive reasons to celebrate.

➤ Instead of being pulled down by all the negative press and TV reporting, stay focused on the activities that bring in the most work, sales or business, then increase those activities

➤ Focus on why you chose to *work from home*

➤ Focus on the benefits you and your family are currently enjoying

➤ Focus on what steps you can take to increase your income or reduce foolish spending

➤ Allow yourself to dream big and work towards that dream

➤ Make sure you look after your health, stress levels and general well being

Priorities

We did look at priorities in Chapter 6, but it is a crucial *money making* tip and worth being mentioned again. How financially successful you and your business are will depend on how good you are at choosing your activities. Not knowing what should be prioritised first will have serious ramifications for your finances.

Here is the all important question you need to ask:

Is what you are doing right now
"Important and Vital" to the success of your finances,
business or career?

If not, why have you chosen that particular task and how can you learn from some of your less than wise decisions. It is an opportunity to strengthen your decision making muscles and get into tip top shape.

The lessons you have learned.

What are the first three action steps you are going to take in order to start saving money?

1._____

_____

_____

_____

2._____

_____

_____

_____

3._____

_____

_____

_____

Checklists

The following lists contain useful items that can help with the smooth set up and efficient running of a home office.

Office equipment ✓

Adequate lighting. ☐

Bookcase. ☐

Clock. ☐

Desk/work station. ☐

Filing cabinet. ☐

Office chair. ☐

Storage units. ☐

Telephone. ☐

Wall notice board. ☐

Additional office equipment for your specific needs ✓

☐

☐

☐

Office supplies ✓

Address labels. ☐

Business cards. ☐

Glue. ☐

Highlighter pens. ☐

House plant. ☐

Letterhead envelopes. ☐

Letterhead paper. ☐

Markers. ☐

Motivational wall hanging. ☐

Packing string. ☐

Packing tape. ☐

Paperclips. ☐

Pencils. ☐

Pens. ☐

Printer cartridges. ☐

Printer paper. ☐

Ring Binder. ☐

Office supplies continued ✓

Rubber bands. ☐

Ruler. ☐

Scissors. ☐

Shredder. ☐

Stamps. ☐

Staple remover. ☐

Stapler. ☐

Staples. ☐

Tape and dispenser. ☐

Various sized envelopes. ☐

Waste basket. ☐

Additional office supplies for your specific needs ✓

☐

☐

☐

☐

Organising products

	✓
Archival storage boxes.	☐
Binder category dividers.	☐
Binders.	☐
Box files.	☐
Business card storage.	☐
Cable tidies.	☐
CD organiser.	☐
Clear binder pockets.	☐
Clear folders.	☐
Desk diary.	☐
Desk top Organiser.	☐
Desktop drawer unit.	☐
Drawer tray.	☐
DVD organiser.	☐
Expanding desk organiser.	☐
Expanding file organiser.	☐
File labels.	☐

Organising products continued

Filing trolley.

Lever arch files.

Letter tray.

Lockable file cabinet.

Magazine files.

Office style cardboard boxes with lid.

Plastic wallets.

Stackable storage cubes.

Suspension files for filing cabinet.

Thick card document wallets.

Under desk drawer storage unit.

Vertical storage holder.

Additional organising products for your specific needs

Useful Contacts

Business advice

Business link

Practical advice and support for business.

www.businesslink.gov.uk

Tel: 0845 600 9 006

Business Support Wales

Flexible support for business: Start Grow Prosper.

www.business-support-wales.gov.uk

Tel: 03000 6 03000

Companies House

The official UK government register of UK companies.

www.companieshouse.gov.uk

Tel: 0303 1234 500

Federation of Small Businesses

The UK's leading Small business advice organisation.

www.fsb.org.uk

Tel: 01253 336 000

Health and Safety Executive

As mentioned in Chapter 2, this is free government advice on health and safety regulations including a specific home working guide.

www.hse.gov.uk

Tel: 0845 345 0055

HM Revenue & Customs

UK tax collection agency.

www.hmrc.gov.uk

Information Commissioner's Office

Data protection information.

www.ico.gov.uk

Tel: 08456 30 60 60

Institute of Chartered Accountants in England and Wales

Accountancy association

www.icaew.co.uk

Tel: 020 7920 8100

Northern Ireland Business Info

Practical advice for Northern Ireland Business

www.nibusinessinfo.co.uk

Tel: 0800 027 0639

National Business Register

Business/domain name, limited company and trademark info with a free on-line name search.

www.start.biz/home.htm

0870 069 9090

Planning Portal

The UK Government's online planning and building regulation resource.

www.planningportal.gov.uk

Scottish Enterprise

Advice on starting and building a business.

www.scottish-enterprise.com

0845 607 8787

UK Intellectual Property Office

Grant IP rights in the UK.

www.ipo.gov.uk

Technology

Nochex

Leading independent UK based online payment company

www.nochex.com

Pay pal

Electronic payment system.

www.paypal.co.uk

08707 307 191

World Pay

Offers internet payment solutions.

www.worldpay.com

0870 366 1290

Never underestimate how important it is for your information to be save and to have a backup, in case your computer crashes.

Microsoft

Data backup made easy.

www.microsoft.com/protect/yourself/data/backup.mspx

Iron Mountain

Off site data storage.

www.ironmountain.co.uk

Communication is key when based at home. Here are a few ideas to help you keep in touch with the outside world.

Skype

Internet phone/video and instant messaging tool.

www.skype.com

Google talk

Chat with family and friends over the internet for free.

www.google.com/talk

Conference Genie

Video and conference facility.

www.conferencegenie.co.uk

0800 012 68 69

Powwow Now

Video and web conferencing, plus the capability for documents to be seen.

www.powwownow.co.uk

020 7990 0900

Huddle

Enables you to create an online environment to securely store files, documents and data. Also manage workflow and share applications across the internet.

www.huddle.net

08709 772 212

Wi-Fi

To escape the potential isolation of your home office, take advantage of several WI-FI locations and enjoy an afternoon working from what I call a 'Café Office'.

BT Openzone

WI-FI hotspots

www.btopenzone.com

0800 169 1397

The Cloud

Wi-Fi Hotspots

www.thecloud.net

My hotspots

Wi-Fi hotspot locator.

www.myhotspots.co.uk

T-Mobile hotspots

Wi-Fi hotspots.

www.t-mobile.co.uk

0800 956 3080

Working from Home organisations

These websites offer advice, information, a chance to ask questions and an opportunity to connect with other individuals who work from home.

Enterprise Nation

A free resource to help you start and grow your business from home.

www.enterprisenation.com

Home Business Alliance

Information to start and grow your own home business.

www.homebusiness.org.uk

Home Business Network

Advice, information and help for home businesses.

www.homebusinessnetwork.co.uk

Remote Employment

Home based and flexible employment solutions.

www.remoteemployment.com

Women in Rural Enterprise (Wire)

Offers business support for women in rural businesses.

www.wireuk.org

Online networking avenues

Ecademy

Connecting business people.

www.ecademy.com

Facebook

Social/business networking site.

www.facebook.com

Linked in

Business networking.

www.linkedin.com

Twitter

Free social messaging.

www.twitter.com

Work from home network

Independent home working portal

www.wfhn.co.uk

Women Unlimited

Online community for female entrepreneurs.

www.women-unlimited.co.uk

Blogs

For the home based entrepreneur, blogs are an effective way to position yourself as an expert and build your reputation.

Blog

UK blog hosting website.

www.blog.co.uk

Blogger

Free blog publishing tool from Google.

www.blogger.com

Blog scene

Blog hosting website.

www.blogscene.co.uk

Thoughts

Conversation engine that connects you with like-minded people.

www.thoughts.com

Word Press

Enables you to work with your blogging software.

www.wordpress.org

Going green

Having a 5 minute commute is not the only way to reduce your carbon emissions and create a greener home office.

Freecycle

Recycle unwanted items to people in your area.

www.uk.freecycle.org

Green works

Giving new life to used office furniture

www.green-works.co.uk

Home recycling

Sells recycle container and gadgets for your home and office.

www.homerecycling.co.uk

08456 123 191

Recycle-More

Recycling advice for your home and office.

www.recycle-more.co.uk

The Carbon Trust

Advice regarding reducing your CO2 footprint.

www.carbontrust.co.uk

0800 085 2005

Home office ideas

Live/Work homes

The UK's live/work property finder.

www.liveworkhomes.co.uk

0845 324 5717

Office POD

The next generation of workplace.

www.officepod.co.uk

Regus

Serviced offices.

www.regus.co.uk

0870 351 9444

Shedworking

A blog for and about home working from a shed.

www.shedworking.co.uk

The home office company

The next generation of workplace.

www.thehomeofficecompany.co.uk

0333 800 5050

Office supplies and furniture

A Place for everything

Innovative storage and organisational products.

www.aplaceforeverything.co.uk

Euro Office

UK's largest supplier of stationery and office supplies online.

www.euroffice.co.uk

0800 316 3876

Flujo

Specialist in home office furniture.

www.flujohome.com

08456 800 224

Ikea

Offers a selection of office and storage products.

www.ikea.com

Staples

Online and store locations that sell office products.

www.staples.co.uk

Viking Direct

An online store for all your office needs.

www.viking-direct.co.uk

Further Reading

Marketing/PR

Duck tape Marketing
The world's most Practical Small Business Marketing Guide.

By: John Jantsch
Publisher: Nelson Business and Imprint of Thomas Nelson
Publishers (2007)
ISBN: 978-1438937533

How to Get Clients to Come to You
A seven–stage system for attracting and keeping clients.

By: Nigel Temple
Publisher: Words at Work; first edition (2007)
ISBN: 978-0955279812

Powerful Marketing On A Shoestring Budget
Over 250 proven, simple and effective marketing tips, tools and strategies that can transform your small business in as little as 28 days.

By: Dee Blick
Publisher: Author house (2008)
ISBN: 978-0785221005

The PR Buzz Factor

How using public relations can boost your business.

By: Russell Lawson
Publisher: Kogan Page (2006)
ISBN: 978-0749444686

This is Social Media

Tweet, blog, link and post your way to business success

By Guy Clapperton
Publisher: Capstone (27 Oct 2009)
ISBN: 978– 1906465704

Twitter Power

How to dominate you market one tweet at a time.

By Anthony Robbins
Publisher: John Wiley & Sons (6 Mar 2009)
ISBN: 978-0470458426

Accounts

Book-Keeping Made Simple

The boogles story.

By Lisa Newton
Publisher: Boogles Ltd (4 Nov 2009)
ISBN: 978-0956425232

Accounts continued...

Keeping Books and Accounts for Small to Medium Size Business

Invaluable information on the process and preparation of accounts, made easy.

By: Colin Richards
Publisher: Emerald Publishing (2008)
ISBN: 978-1847160898

Keeping it Simple

Small business bookkeeping, self-assessment and VAT.

By: James Smith
Publisher: Taxcafe UK Limited (2008)
ISBN: 978-1904608820

Mastering Book-Keeping

A complete guide to business accounting.

By: Peter Marshall
Publisher: How to Books Ltd (2009)
ISBN: 978–1845283247

Tax without Tears

Tax and accounts for the self-employed working from home.

By Robert Sherwood
Publisher: Filament Publishing (2010)
ISBN: 978-1905493296

Inspirational reading

Feel the Fear and Do it Anyway
How to turn your fear and indecision into confidence and action.

By: Susan Jeffers
Publisher: Vermilion (4 Jan 2007)
ISBN: 978-0091907075

How to Win Friends and Influence People
A no-nonsense guide to being a better person.

By Dale Carnegie
Publisher: Vermilion; New edition (19 May 2006)
ISBN: 978-0091906818

How to Instantly Connect with Anyone
96 All-new little trick for big success in every social and business situation.

By: Leil Lowndes
Publisher: Vermilion (1 Jul 2010)
ISBN: 978–0091935443

Louder Than Words
Take your career from average to exceptional with the hidden power of nonverbal intelligence.

By Joe Navarro
Publisher: Harper Business (19 Apr 2010)
ISBN: 978-0061771392

The Power of No
Take back your life with a two-letter word.

By: Beth Wareham
Publisher: Hay House UK (4 Jan 2010)
ISBN: 978-1848501812

Home Office design ideas

At Work, at home
Design ideas for your home workspace.

By Neal Zimmerman
Publisher: Taunton Press inc (25 Apr 2002)
ISBN: 978-1561583799

Building the Custom Home Office
Projects for the complete home work space.

By: Niall Barrett
Publisher: Taunton Press inc (17 Oct 2002)
ISBN: 978–1561584215

Live/Work
Working at home , living at work.

By Deborah K Dietsch
Publisher: Harry N Abrams (5 May 2008)
ISBN: 978-0810994003

Shedworking
The alternative workplace revolution.

By: Alex Johnson
Publisher: Frances Lincoln (3 Jun 2010)
ISBN: 978-0711230828

Small Office Home Office
Architecture details.

By: Monsa Editoriale team
Publisher: Instituto Monsa de Ediciones (1 May 2008)
ISBN: 978-8496823372

About Purely Peppermint and Your Author

Rachael Ross is the founder of Purely Peppermint.com

A unique consultancy providing specialist services that enables individuals and organisations to develop cost efficient and highly effective home working environments.

She works with individuals, small organisations and large businesses by providing practical solutions that are tailor made for each environment.

Using hands-on practical support, Rachael strives for clients to have the greatest of success in their chosen field. She ensures that their home office environment is improved to create the ideal setting for each individual to achieve just that success. Rachael uses her design training and creativity to see the potential in an office space, even when all a client sees is clutter. There isn't as aspect of working from home that she isn't willing to tackle, some of which are covered in this book, plus much, more.

Client follow-up consists of telephone advice combined with leadership training so that the environment is maintained and enhanced to cope with the inevitable changes that all successful businesses and home workers go through.

As a regular contributor to leading UK working from home websites and magazines Rachael has been invited to the Home Business Summit at the House of Commons, London to advise central government on potential improvements regarding the support they offer home businesses.

Rachael speaks passionately on the subject of becoming organised whilst working from home and is invited regularly to speak at many conferences and seminars that are now highlighting the benefits of establishing a home business. No one leaves these events without having a few sparkling ideas on how to become much more effective when working from home.

Rachael Ross

www.purelypeppermint.com